T H E S

E **INT**

RICA

CIES

The Poiema Poetry Series

Poems are windows into worlds; windows into beauty, goodness, and truth; windows into understandings that won't twist themselves into tidy dogmatic statements; windows into experiences. We can do more than merely peer into such windows; with a little effort we can fling open the casements, and leap over the sills into the heart of these worlds. We are also led into familiar places of hurt, confusion, and disappointment, but we arrive in the poet's company. Poetry is a partnership between poet and reader, seeking together to gain something of value—to get at something important.

Ephesians 2:10 says, "We are God's workmanship . . ." *poiema* in Greek—the thing that has been made, the masterpiece, the poem. The Poiema Poetry Series presents the work of gifted poets who take Christian faith seriously, and demonstrate in whose image we have been made through their creativity and craftsmanship.

These poets are recent participants in the ancient tradition of David, Asaph, Isaiah, and John the Revelator. The thread can be followed through the centuries—through the diverse poetic visions of Dante, Bernard of Clairvaux, Donne, Herbert, Milton, Hopkins, Eliot, R. S. Thomas, and Denise Levertov—down to the poet whose work is in your hand. With the selection of this volume you are entering this enduring tradition, and as a reader contributing to it.

—D.S. Martin
Series Editor

"This collection of elemental Kentucky poems will land 'like starlight in your throat.' You will want to sing Dave Harrity aloud to find that "words have wombs," that what he calls the dusk in our bodies, our 'cairns of guilt,' still birth and mark dim paths of light. *These Intricacies* will clear a way into your own and leave you grateful for each twist and sudden turn. Like St. Augustine, 'Take and read.'"

—Paul Willis
author of *Say This Prayer into the Past*

"In these poems, Dave Harrity invites us—into the poems, yes, but also into thought and quiet and a contemplative solitude rare in our century. Here is a poet attentive to the worlds beyond us and the worlds within us. Here are poems that appreciate creation's perfection and life's imperfection. *These Intricacies* reveals stars and stone walls and kitchen windows—those things I thought I already knew—with unfamiliar and welcome clarity."

—Lynn Domina
author of *Framed in Silence*

"Intricate only begins to describe the delicate, strong, interlaced qualities of Dave Harrity's poems. Because he values this world in all its complexity, Harrity refuses to reduce any part of creation to a single feature. Each poem here is a complex weaving of poetic attention—image, voice, line, diction, and, especially, tone—into an honest, lamenting, desiring voice that embodies the human necessity 'to turn away the dark, / to call down light from stars.'"

—David Wright
author of *The Small Books of Bach* and *A Liturgy for Stones*

"Dave Harrity metes out his keen sense of our material reality in *These Intricacies* with an undeniable spirit-eye: a gun shop houses beasts, the throat starlight; guilt builds a little cairn, belief a hand of wings; the body makes room for dusk but cannot deny its uncertain history—those 'many accidents it took to make this skin.' I'm punctured by all that's hallowed and harsh in these poems. What's more: I'm thankful."

—Susanna Childress
author of *Jagged with Love* and *Entering the House of Awe*

"Dave Harrity's *These Intricacies* is a welcomed new voice in American poetry for the muscle and soul and lyric vision it offers us. Not may poets today will write a long, complex line of questioning, digging, and seeking visceral answers to spiritual questions, ways to bury doubt or reveal belief, as Harrity does. His point of view as a young man, a husband, father, teacher, and above all a seeker of truth in our very human contemporary lives, is one I recommend to you through these poems. The comfort and confidence I feel in his lines reminds me of mid-twentieth-century voices such as a Richard Hugo, James Wright, and John Anderson with the Songs of David weaving throughout. Harrity is an original who wants to know, fights to understand the world he finds himself in, and this is the driving engine of his poetics. There is nothing fragmented or partial here, no blurts of thought, but kneaded considerations few poets take the time to write these days. When he says 'I'll grind the grain if it means I'll see your face,' I feel his love for his tortured fellow humans, and I know that turning anywhere in this book, I will find an answer, even if buried deep. I highly recommend, especially to our younger generation of poets, Dave Harrity's poetry which has something to say that is real, substantial, and above all uplifting in a time when we need this so."

—Jeanie Thompson
author of the forthcoming *The Myth of Water: Poems from the Life of Helen Keller*

THES EINT RICA CIES

Dave Harrity

CASCADE *Books* • Eugene, Oregon

THESE INTRICACIES

The Poiema Poetry Series

Cascade Books
An Imprint of Wipf and Stock Publishers
199 W. 8th Ave., Suite 3
Eugene, OR 97401

www.wipfandstock.com

ISBN 13: 978-1-4982-3693-5

Cataloging-in-Publication data:

Dave Harrity.

    These Intricacies / Dave Harrity.

    58 p. + ix ; 23 cm—

    The Poiema Poetry Series

    ISBN 13: 978-1-4982-3693-5

    1. American Poetry—21st Century I. Title II. Series

PS3725.A237 2015

Manufactured in the USA.

For Amanda, Emmalynne, & Gabriel—still our lives.

Contents

1/

1/

NAMING THE STARS

To know that there's room enough for dusk in the body,
step out in open air and breathe—the day downing.
What it is to end is what begins us each time over.

A walk to think it over—the hour when day slips off
and crumples like the linen of a summer dress
to reveal the forms that humble us.

There's a word to say for each imperfection we possess,
for failures making good on even smaller promises,
to beat back times we entertain our little wrongs.

And what it must be like to turn away the dark,
to call down light from stars—poverties we have
hung bare, a constant grain for each of these mistakes.

IN JANUARY

There are words I seem to only say with you,
but I try to pray in spite of that. I say them
as I walk this cut bank by the creek,
as the morning's ice storm shines
like all the words you use to talk to God.
I bow to silver trees, to white fire glazing bright
and what the new snow hides beneath—
shallow water soon to feed the fields, green
born from a melt of sleet. This is how
the things of earth put away the past:
it's another diagnosis, another glum return
from sickness. I want to have good words
to say to you when I come home, but seem
stuck on the differences between a quiet
and a silence: that what finds its way to voice
with us hopes for more than spent uncertainty
and the ceaseless, steady thaw of my belief.

THE JILTED HUSBAND SPEAKS

What comes forward from darkened fields this winter? How long
can we deceive ourselves? Cold, true like a stray dog, nuanced
like a gossip's words. Should we try to make it through another winter?

Drifts and pulp-white sweeps, sleet cuts into dirty snow—
we're baubles packed in antique curios, rising early
to battered banks and crystal trees, teeth brushed white as winter.

Our mix—bitter bickering or loathing's hollow swell. And when you
touch my hand in bed the only thing I know is how to melt away,
as you'll return to his front door—shadowbox, weaving winter.

Constellations tell this one each night. Graffito fixed above,
ages spent retelling songs. The lie rehearsed till vivid and complete.
Corvus, fly away or hold your stupid tongue this winter.

Our minds arrayed in hail and damages—shut-ins to the storm
and servants to the haze. Choking down dull serial, swallowing
equal parts discomfort and disdain when we touch once all winter.

In the dusky park's bright snow, I walk into the storm: frantic white,
orange lamp-lit prints, my squeaking boots. We are both
the pond and ice, both the street and filthy slush of moonless winter.

My body's built of frozen earth and yours from mine. We've dressed up
our disgust with self-doubt. Incriminate myself again? I speak nothing,
wishing I could turn the bare skin of my back away from winter.

SLAVE WALL

Along that dusted drag, cut through the thicket, rise slabs
of stacked stones from some hundred years ago.
The craggy course lurching farther than my eye allows—
dead arrangements with the past and harder truths piled
to the knee, defying budding cramps of thorny weeds
and stretching like a snake dividing lines of property.
This records the era's cruel, brutal trade—blind power
eating at the heart. How does a wall get made into an altar?
Which fractured rock reminds us of the hate we hide away?
Each rugged memory of history's chains, each raw split
making known the past. And this is how we go about
remembering it here: Kentucky River to county line,
we tally up the evil heaped, stone by daunting stone.

THE HOLE

I remember your face surprised
at what was missing
as we stood at Ground Zero,
looking in Manhattan's mouth.
The buildings on the block
still draped in sheets, frocked statues.
Rain and mist arriving with us
to fill the gap and soak our coats.
You said *I love you,* and I thought
how strange and sudden we can be.

What comes after a moment
when you're still and staring?
Tragedy made us hungry and dumb—
a long walk and night ferry home,
clicking photos of the cityscape,
absent two jeweled reaches to the sky.

What should have come,
and what comes in the distance,
is that we're hardly more
than intimate strangers, and I
should have said it back.

But there were sounds
I couldn't make then and the ones
we heard had to be enough—
taxis bleating out, flags clapping
deep above our heads, boots
against the ground. I said
nothing back, and now
there's nothing but a hole
in me, fathomed with regret.

CONTEMPLATING THE EGG

If it's blamelessness you want, stay in bed.
At the moment you crack an egg you've sinned.

As what's careless and rote—a state, a taking place—
will open. The egg will crackle

its hundred laughed hellos at your thoughtless repetition.
And you won't hear since you're so busy

planning the day, your simple indestruction. Impervious begins
your wrong turns and you forget

this has to end, that this might be the last thing that you kill—
finality cradled in the hand,

what small oval and your hunger for the inside. All of it
coming out so easily: you

flick your wrist and let the day begin.

MY GRANDFATHER SINGS AGAIN

I found a cassette with your voice singing.
The wheels of the tape turned away from time
to let me hear your rendition of *Folsom Prison Blues*.
When I was a boy, I sat on your lap and you taught
me those words—the song of a lonely prisoner staring
from his cell window at the miles of rail that ran
the train past the jail. When I was a boy, the dollar bill
woven in your strings was a rattling snare of steam.
When I was a boy, your voice was the wheel grinding
the track, rolling through California. But now
you sing to me and I'm the prisoner listening
to a whistle blow the warm swell of being free.
I'm watching the train's slow escape, soot billow
falling to earth as a frown of black cloud.

ATROPOS

That we pretend to be enlightened in this life
is a mystery all its own. I myself have wondered
many times about the shadows made by fire,
dancing on the dark walls of a cave, or how to
measure increments of pleasure with numeric might—
apparently some guys work round the clock
on stuff like this, but no one's close to any kind
of answer. And that's what's strange about this side
of time—fixations on breaking bolts holding back
the mind. There's a quote or two about it that I know.
One goes, *I think therefore I am*, and people seem
to like the ring of that, but such intelligence
can make it tough to see the truth, since innocence
can be its own discovery, or existence of anything
at all a delusion of what one thinks or hopes
to be. And is being actually a thing we can believe?
This mulling over quality has wandered far enough.
I say let the tissue-membrane marinade keep still,
silent-soaking in the skull, largely undisturbed—
bulb without a hum, hush of cinders fading out.
Because this year I did it to myself again—
got lost in too much thinking—the dust and ash
of looking at the pavement and facades instead
of really touching earth—only seeing forests in
the trees inside my head and giving narrow answers
like *yes, no, today,* and *tomorrow*. All tinged
with careful certainty. No bulwark *maybes*,
or thoughtful *mights*—no bombastic *let-me-think-
about-its*. I want replies so simple that they keep
away the tragedies of gun-smoke gray and let me rest.
Then yesterday a boy I knew died at his own hand.
I thought harder than I'd ever thought before, so hard
to wish it all away. And all I understood was how
simple is the loss: a cord, a garage rafter. No moving

parts or any explanation. No clarifying note or
angsty teenage cry for help. Austere as pinching
snipped threads of his life and putting out the fires
in his wake, the ones that eat at us when someone
goes away like that. If you ask me, it all comes down
to this: we want a haven in the head, if only for a day—
a place of rest and home for the unease of memory,
an infirmary where lives can't waste and thinking
gets you far enough away from what ugliness you see—
some hiddenness with no boys holding their uncertainties,
bound tight and cold with accidental grays.

THE SHUTTLE

The news was clear about the tragedy:
they found a wedding band in Texas dirt,
finger still stuck in like a nut around a bolt.
Locals went walking, looking for more wreck—

patches, metal, jumpsuits singed, and scraps.
On TV, the president said to watch the sky,
and look heavenward just like Isaiah did.
Some saw the streak of smoke left lingering,

trekking through the vivid blue of day.
I did my best to lift my eyes in hope,
wondering if they could see the moon or
had time enough to pray before the blast.

All I could see were white animal faces
rolling off clouds, looking down at me.

AT CAVE HILL CEMETERY

Some say a beginning, others an end. Either way,
we are a window into earth: starched and quiet slate
of monuments, eroded annunciation of an angel's face.

The graves are tidy, arranged repetitions for miles
in magnolias. We are quiet, reminded: bustled jars against
the former lives and sparrows arrowing over the lake.

The answers are buried, and we wander. You wonder
if any of it ends. All leaves waxing out, seeded reds
shelling skins. Beneath ground, all touch is nothing.

No caravan of clouds above crosses—no blank or gray
or white winnowed with speech. Our voices: slight lisps
to one another in the twisting blond exit of summer.

NORTHERN CROSS

It hangs steady, leaning like the shoulder
of the man releasing breath from his body.
I make my own cloud that goes up,

away into the crisp night, lost in blue branches.
One more story gets untold and dissipates,
strung unseen in the small complexities we've retold

for centuries, what we've written into light.
Blessed shapes or beaming eyes—I keep learning
how to see them right, believe the brilliance they divide.

WHERE SHADOWS COME FROM

So simple a small thing as light, as what travels to you
when you're half asleep above the things you tuck away—

the slight and hidden past, where your father seems to live
remembered in old photographs and letters, back behind

dumbbell resolutions and gathered dust. One day you decide
to reach to him, pull out his life and remind you how it matters.

Look into it, eye to eye with the man who made you,
right before he left. Are there promises made in giving life,

that even a son must say the past he doesn't know back
to himself and dream what was once his making?

To hold the light he did—dull-edged shadow of your tiny hand—
again, the two of you are left sitting, touchless in the dark.

FATHOM

You can't escape your blood
and all the sins that flow from it—
your father's bastard father whose
father only came around when he
was hungry for food or sex.
                              He'd eat
and fork the branches of the family tree,
splicing wholes to halves. Or think of it like this:
he threw a line from his body
like translucent fishing wire to plunk
against the water and dive the distance
of the future.
                    You thought you
were special, thought this was a gift.
You thought you could drag your weight
from bed each day and go into the world.
What do you know about yourself?
You packed boxes years ago and moved
into this house.
                        You're an uncertain history.
Like me and every neighbor that you have.
Some big bang and far-flung matter,
swaddled in a cozy swirl of gravity
and beaten out to life.
                              How many accidents
it took to make this skin? How many times
did fathers dig hands into the earth
to pull back root or stone?
Intricate allowances. This blood
disease. Punches to your jaw
pulled back. So many shots fired
into her just so you could crawl?
                              Something can't come

14

from nothing. You are no exception, not immune.
You will be a father. You will be hungry.
You will cleave the tree to make
some accident.
                    You will sink
deep enough to prove
the rule.

YOU ARE SITTING IN THE KITCHEN, ONLY A WITNESS

On the table, the man cleans a gun.
A boy aside—pajamas and a ragged rabbit,
stuffed and sewn with button eyes.

The boy begins to cry, though he can't name
a reason yet. The man hands the boy
a cloth and swabs and oil can. Grunts instruction.

This kind of man cuts away all color
from his life, restrained fever in monochrome,
blind to all his accidents.

This kind of boy falls less in love
With what can be imagined. His clothes grow
smaller every day, slinking off his frame.

The double-barrel's obtuse ends,
the laid out elements—all lead-ready, clean.
And from here things move fast.

Shriek of metal on metal, a clack together.
The man's voice a trigger squeezed, the boy's desire
something like a dove. A hammer and a shell.

Now past the clumsiness of destiny
and onto brighter things: swilled chirps
of crickets in the field, under summer stars,

gloved and silken silhouettes, overgrown grass
popping seed. What noises shape our small sobriety?
Strung serendipities no one can explain.

LOVING THY NEIGHBOR

Baking bread, I've run out of flour, so I go
door-to-door to ask for what I need. I've stirred up
enough gall to stand on your stoop. All this audacity
I have made moot when I can't hear your walking
to the door or looking through the glass or sliding back
the chain to welcome me. All this audacity made moot
by what's in me that leavens then recedes, that when
I come to you, I rarely want to hear the things you say.
I'm sure you understand such a creatured thing—
the asking, that is. The way I come to you, whipping up
metaphors to symbol out a truth, to circumstance
and qualify my process or the means? But all I want
is flour now, and I'll be on my way. Sure, I've heard
the rumors—people saying you are dead—but that
seems harder to believe than other things I've heard.
And if you're dead it surely isn't news—we killed you
long before and now we've just begun to see. Perhaps
you're smaller than you were before—emaciate from
growing old, slighter each square you tear back from the year.
Once so monolithic but now a grouch retiree—a *tchotchke*
we've corralled into a hutch, some trinket possibility.
It's what you were that's harder to imagine: wings
and robes turned pillboxed medicines, clouds and tongues
of fire turned tepid water ringed grimy in a tub. You know
I've been around the block enough to understand
the tragedy of lonely widows, pregnant teens. I've seen
the evidence we're leveling and it's not too pretty. Hell,
I'm part of it myself. But friend, can you get up
one more time and let me know you're there? I'll grind
the grain if it means I'll see your face, like your body traded
for my offering—to a neighbor who has moved or is asleep,
or fallen down and needs help getting up, or sleeps without
a breath. But I hope you're waiting for a visitor, maybe
breathing deeper than you ever were before. And I'm here now,

an old friend, to catch your breath, and brush your teeth,
and dress you up, and sit and hold your hand.

ETYMOLOGY

Try to remember what he taught: find North in stars,
drive a nail, or clench a fist and follow through against
the iron of a cheekbone. You may have been a boy,
but you remember all these things passing through
the town where he was born—ragged holler of coal,
a life between the whistle trills. So much even that
whenever you hear the word *Kentucky,* your memory
claps on and he's looking at you to decide. All those
syllables throbbing one sound. He read aloud to show
you words have wombs and modulate from names
to places, suffixed with identities. He told you stories
of a man who walked far enough into the woods
to make a name and life, so that word never goes
unnoticed. Even now *Kentucky* glows a wanderlust,
it's home cradled in the ribs, make a fist the way he did,
stand square and say it, fight your way to make it through.

ON PRAYER #1

Who walks away holding the pieces of my life?
Are these petitions signs of desire or disease?
Will they ever grow into something I can touch?

A darkness, a trumpet, a tempest, a fire—
ingredients with hope to make an easier belief.
No—simply moving pieces of my life.

And what comes of all these prayers?
Gales of whispers ransoming release—
acceptable necessities, never needing touch.

What I make in darkness despises light so much—
doubt refusing, doubt against the one who speaks.
Can I walk away with any peace in my life?

Set aside the scripts—piecemeal voice,
guilt's dusty hands brushed clean.
I want my prayer to be close to touch.

Lord, divide my simple words and see—
shake promises, mistake my awe for reverence.
I'm stepping back cradling the pieces of my life,
but will you become a body I can touch?

2/

NOVENA

1/

Salvation captured in stained glass:
oranges burn to reds,

scarlets into navy blues—
all one shining mosaic.

Thin rivulets of solder snake
the edges of each sliver,

binding them together—
glass in quiet collision.

You hang like a withered vine—
arms stretched out just so,

wide chevron flex of your elbow
and the milky skin of your hands,

tipped by sooted nails,
embrace pins to hold you in place

above the pews, against the echoes
of my footsteps in this vaulted room.

How I want to hold you up so you can breathe.
I want to love you like these windows

love light, or the way the thief on your right
will ask to be with you in paradise.

If I accept your images—
passion born in tesserae of sun—

can I believe your voice
is not the groan of wind outside

but the hush bowed in breath
before you say my name?

2/

Having faith is hard
when every part of you

drowns in the water
of one freighted word: *believe*.

I want to divide you
with smaller syllables,

as water separates
two scapes of land.

I should learn to
let the current sift

and silt my weary body.
I should learn to float

to you so we won't be
separate shores curving

with the river. But I can't
maintain the strokes

to beat the rushing tow,
can't recall belief enough

to make my body move,
belief enough for my feet

to cut the water. And though
I see you swim the river now,

it's the rescue I can't contend:
your breathless lap will lead to me,

you'll look into my face
and see that I'm afraid—

deceived—without faith enough
to try. From my mouth

you'll hear the curse—
two halves, my lies—goodbye.

3/

Spring came
for two weeks

then buried the new life:
snow over stone

and killing every bloom.
Your way to remind us

that death is just
another word

for patience
and patience

just another word
for helping me forget?

Your work is so slow
that I can never see

what you're making
without impatience

breaking through
and taking root,

loyal bud jutting
just enough to

frustrate belief.
And I go on withering,

thinking spring's arrival
will be soon. What's left

of you across the ground—
puddled in the ebbing cold

or frozen rain—not winter
still, and not quite spring.

Why keep striking down
what starts to live?

I want you to be
green, seasonless:

no sinking back
to bare and bleak,

no holding back the light.
So split our seeds

and break the ground
and call back life

with sun enough to
warm and startle us.

4/

Every time I try to pray,
I'm looking to the sky

where three blackbirds
spiral into the sun's searing eye.

All the shapes and motions:
weightless bodies, tips of wings

swallowed in a yellow soak
until they disappear, hidden in

a flash so hot and sudden
that I must turn my eyes

quickly to the ground,
remembering there are gazes

bright and furious, graces
burning me to look away.

5/

Dad told it like a fairy tale—ancient eyes
searching for a boy with a forgotten face.

The thousand look to you then lift you high
if you can catch just one light in your hands...

So I'd chase the wandering little bugs,
sweltered lulling in the half-lit dusk.

Their weightless flight—tiny hulls
floating from the grass and out of reach.

Why didn't you bring one home?
And I'd have no answer in me,

instead this little cairn of guilt—
one that's made me keep belief

in what I only saw for seconds
as it rose up from my life. This light

on and off, morse in heat-blue haze,
elusive bug climbing to fainter stars.

My god, I'm still the boy walking
through the field of summer dark,

the one who's reaching for our void,
trying hard to hold a fading light

6/

Let me know the distance
from your ghost to my bones.

Let these knees singe the ground
under coal-brushed clouds.

Let my voice grow into prayer
with my face against the soil.

Let the seed begin the tree,
the taproot kiss through stone.

Let hands grow to branches,
divide and rise to green.

Let fingers flower into leaves
and wander to the sky.

Let churning be an icon,
the beginning to your reach.

Let rain create the heat
and batter every leaf.

Let lines of lightning chalk the sky,
fierce flare to flash and rush.

Let my pieces smolder
in the absence of your touch.

7/

What do I know of offering? I have nothing to give you
but the same weary words, hollow hands, worn creases.

To believe. To believe in what it means to be apart—to believe
in the weight of weaknesses. You should know that I will learn

to find you, that I'm gathering
your images together, all the scattered pieces

of your face. My palms wait to be filled,
to pull you from earth's black soil.

You are every word I want to know.
My hands opening like wings

to pump: again
and again to

believe.

8/

I will open my hands to learn
about offering—that I

must trade my dry body for your
living water—all ten fingers joined

together reliving my sin. I am
a tired pilgrim confessing, always

trying to swallow what you've poured
into the broken bowl of my hands.

9/

I wonder if belief
is walking by sound

and not by sight,
because this morning

I went out,
houses still dark,

and shut my eyes.
One bird called

into the cold.
Another answered.

Then another, until
a singular sound

opened to the ring
of thousands.

Every starling
murmuration

lifting to one
song of ascent.

My eyes open
to the empty field—

a prayer for sight
in every single sound

that blooms
from you.

3/

ON PRAYER #2

What was that? Rabbit flashing frantic in
yogic silence—the slightest hair of motion
is a suite played with pots and spoons,

a daisy chain of images every time
you're still. You love the miracle of being clever
too much to unpack the soul, box by box.

Fibonaccied from your concentration,
like snails and their coy eyes, filaments
electric with your own significance:

blinking to shift your focus from the fact
your mind's arranged like gaudy furniture.
Flash and singe, the glaring off

so you can see the kitsch that's gathered
in your drawer. Use a safety pin to latch words
sweet together. Easily the mind lumbers

with distractions, red-herring convalescence.
What about silence asks to be filled up?
What about silence asks to be filled up?

Now, the shock of current in your hamstring
all the way up your side. Shadow-making
then shadow-breaking. Your light dimmed.

Coins roll away, sheep go scattered—forgetting
why it was you came again in quiet. What
small rumbles in your living get washed away—

wave pulled back slowly to the sea,
wave kicked up and sunken with your sleep.
What to do but pick up your mat and walk.

WAS BLIND

This morning a spider crawled beneath a clover
twice its size—nature saying everything it could.

All hidden and knit—no dust of progress, clutch
of earth—the patience of release. Our lives

keep beginning to matter, all of us meeting
one another a second time. Sun comes forward,

fluffed columbine later in the year. Before that,
snow sadly rehearses that it is only water.

These seasons remain as all we are, but we
hold up what we make instead: lengths

reminding us that being still is natural, banners
held high saying we've loved one another since birth,

by words we haven't made with our mouths
but by our hands. He descended from his web,

swaddling his next nourishment—he weaves, suspends,
and crawls off full again. The reason you are here,

the reason you've arrived so sweetly at the flickering
now—what to count, what to count forward or back?

What wasn't said matters so little now that you
easily forgive the stars for turning out their eyes.

HALLELUJAH, I'M A BUM

I was told the way to water: go down to the river to pray.
And so I did—followed the highway till a bridge emerged.
It wasn't easy, but I took the hill carefully and stumbled.
I took the hill not knowing what to look for—not knowing
if our paths would cross. I should have seen it coming:
graffiti, dilapidated couches, cans of beer and rubber scrap.
Not so much surprised as let down—a stop for mendicants
or rebel teens: nothing really mystical, no elegance or majesty—
just a silent mucked-on river moving slow. Bored and disappointed,
I started cataloging junk—the litter and the rocks—thinking salvation
might arrive. But damn—it took so long my beard grew and an itch
to wander. But you already know that don't you, friend?
Already know the time we waste seduced by possibility
of change—wishing for a vision instead of simply taking in
a scene. Yes, I got tired. Yes, I sat down in the ashes and dust
of the given day with no one around to see me cry. Human, I know,
but so is counting I suppose. I wondered what it must be like
when snow settles on the river here, the canopy of bare trees there—
I imagined all the seasons that I'd missed before I came,
the little ways we measure out the life: skimmed waterbugs,
cattail cloak, leaves blundering their color to recede—
anything, really, to semaphore an evidence that things stay
as they're made. There's joy in knowing everything evolves—
that even you must sing a different song to each stone buried
under sand, to every animal teeming in the water. And the garbage
that we make even has it's place upon the shore—sandy filters
crunched against the curb, bottle caps, and dull glass: every little thing
accounted for and placed. I was so relieved with revelation
I reclined across the busted couch and picked my fingernails, and read
the writing on the wall. Above me droned the intermittent cars, rolling
their engagements to the future, cargo carried over bridge, taxied
to unknown destinations and people without names. And I wondered
who might let me hitch and where I might be going next.

TRIGGER

Moments before I open the door to B.C.'s Firearms I hesitate
since I've never really held a gun. And now they're glaring
at me under glass. The store quiet but for the clerk in the corner
and outside rain, a bullet-holed metal sign says, *Homeland Security*
is YOUR Responsibility! I can't even begin to know
what to do or say in a place like this, but can't deny the gravity and pull.

Last week, the small-town paper had concerning words: . . . *woman pulled*
into an alley . . . and . . . *left for dead . . .* You put the paper down, hesitated
speaking. And that fear all rushed back, a silently articulated pulse. I know
you well enough to feel what happens when a man holds you in his glare
and eyes you like a steak. I know my hate alone can't make you secure—
that what I carry with me can't reverse being backed into a corner.

But here I am learning about different kinds of pistols, leaning over the
corner of the case displays. I pick a short-snouted one, aim the barrel, pull
the stem, and fire dry—*click.* It startles me. I hold it still, clutched secure
like a baseball, skin gleaming in the satin finish. I hesitate
to try again. Daunting lockwork fixed behind my mirrored glare
in heavy steel. The clerk comes back to fill me in on what I don't know.

I once asked my father if he ever had one tucked away we didn't know
about, hidden in a closet or some forgotten corner
of our house. *I never felt I needed one,* he says, and sends a stiff-eyed glare
my way. *But what if you had?* I say. He thinks before he speaks, pulling
together a rightness in his words. *I wouldn't even hesitate—*
I'd do anything for us, to make this family secure.

The clerk says to me: *You gotta squeeze—keep that wrist straight and secure.*
My fingers tighten round the grip, steadying the weight. I know
how it will feel, it's strange—*click.* The sharp sound of no hesitation.
Now if you wanna guard the home and such, this is it. But don't feel cornered
to buy a thing just yet since we got plenty here to see. But I can't pull
my mind from thoughts of you afraid and what I can't do—it's glaring.

This feeling in me can't quite find a name, but grins slight when I glare
past the muzzle's shadowed eye. What wouldn't I do for your security?
And this is doubt ending in a recklessness—for you I want to pull
the hammer back, let a bullet shred the air. A salvo's knowing
red response, guardian afraid of what might be—corners
of this odd anxiety allowed and lit, altars where I lay my hesitation.

Can I pull another thing for ya? The beast goes back—secure, boxed.
I glare to the window near the corner, the storm still spitting rain.
And then my voice, no hesitation: *you know how much this one will cost me?*

TO MARK THE PLACE

Remember I said this:
the day may be beginning
where belief will end.

Looking back, how would you define it now?
A life revealed in clarity of morning prayer:
scape of dawn, stars receding in thin cloud,
the body bent—request or resignation?

Even if you don't, stars understand.
Lights arrive because their bodies
are already gone—graves always give way to glory.
As if the dark stones over their violet tombs
have rolled back and it's now enough
to make you see what little faith you had before.

Isn't this your devotion?
Place your hand in your pocket
when asked to give.
Give whatever it is you find there.

And if you should pull a dry seed
place it in the earth.
Forget it came from you.
Never let your left hand know.

Years from now, following home
those tiny lights on some long road back to this place,
you might be surprised to see
your forgotten gift revising the horizon—
small green proof that we were here,
that we once crossed this road together.

No record of denials set down;
no crowing uncertainties about it.
And what you once thought anathema
turned into the kindness of incantation.

Maybe what I said before was wrong:
the day is actually ending
where this world will not believe.

CONFESSION

Walking in the morning, I was
the only one awake.

Kids down the block, waiting.
Kids eating breakfast, tying up

their shoes and out the door.
The air nips at all of us on any

given day. But it's the sound
I walk for: singing and piano keys

when she thinks no one is listening.

NATURAL ORDER

If you're paying attention, you may notice
the way all things move around you,
but there are no guarantees.

You can't remember childhood—so you stand
in another's memory, silent movie
turning back on itself. You begin
to learn a language that's always lived in you.

Then as a teenager, everything is wrong—
endings of your life all too common.
Will you ever ask the right questions?

You leave home—parents anxious and aware.
As boy meets girl, all moves
forward without ever moving a frame.

You get married.
You fall in love.

You bring a child into a world you think you understand,
but you're always wrong about certainty.
Then comes the night when you walk into and away
from yourself at the same time:

holding that familiar hand—children having gone
the way you went away—you look up:
that starry helm turning all these years behind a shroud.

One light you do not remember being there,
pulsing little pearl.
You're slow enough to wonder
what you might have missed.

And you ask it to fall, so you can wish
this life to live again all over.

GHOST STORY

You were thirteen when the carnival came to town.
A girl on the bus ride home from school loaned you
her favorite book—Ghost Stories—and wrote her address
in careful ink over the title page. She lived nearby.

That afternoon you pedaled to her house. She never
saw you, never looked up from her book—her windows
always paper, never glass. At school, she asked to meet
at the gates—is there anything to say but yes?

The wheel stood high and bright over the ground, wrung
calliope notes between mechanical starts. You rode together
again and again, early autumn cool ribboning out over town,
silver wave and mirrored twilight. The woodmill lights confused

with low-set stars, the bucket rocked like a chime.
How simple the crowd moving below, how simple the music
sputtering to sink. She asked if you believe in ghosts.
What was it you said? Light on her hair, honey-cheeked.

The way she said ghost made you want to believe.
Now it all grows to shadow, doesn't it? Memory losing
what it once held close. How exactly does it end? As if you can
cup your hands to drink—water leaking out around the knuckles.

Her face is clear in shy freckles, the wheel is clinking up.
None of that matters now: when you answered she took your hand.

FROM THE HAMMOCK

The wind is
a cradle held

in the long trees
and they swing,

soft and tired,
staffs parting

a bright sea,
this transom

between what's
heaven crossed by

what's less than
heaven—belly

of the sky
brushed clean.

QUANTA

Here is one thing I think I know:
each voice a variation of one inflection,
singular instinct, singular image.

As today, flustered movements of birds
and leaves, children running in twilight autumn.

And it was years ago together, dianthus dusk
against the exact silver of a hospital bed,
such a pinkish sleep in intimacy,
in the strangeness of mother and child.

Something like starlight in the throat,
something like silence realized as a friend.
It's best to keep this near the surface, a mode
of you I try to understand.

Sun and circuit, the constant downing,
paper doll precise, clipped shadows' long array
in each exchange—birds in tenuous corkscrew
moan to blue apogee in air, back dive back.

What is there that stays this way? Whole as
a boy and a girl laughing through motion, light
bound open from their bodies.

BLUEGRASS WINTER VIEW

Winter brings a quiet kind of storm—
a soundless scape framed by our front window.
We have watched the movement over
the field, still sky fixed white and gray.

So far we've traveled this year, and I'm wanting
summer: hot breeze thick with sweat and oak leaves,
the body's slow dance with pollen. At night,
the sky open and settled, flecks above us.

I once read that if Earth moved a foot
from it's rotation that we'd freeze, plunge
into a new Ice Age. Funny to think of such a thing—
inches from a season instead of days.

Winter fades, of course, but now we watch
each familiar thing cover and dissolve.
If I press my ear to the glass, I can hear
there is a sound ice makes as it hits the house.

PANTOUM BREAKFAST SCRAMBLE

This routine is now your life: pen, paper, morning light.
You see all the early hours—bright head of cresting sun;
the world outside lit and lingering beyond the glass.
You watch shadows on the floor—sure, crawling, alive.

Seen ahead, the sun-crested early hours, you bridle.
The din of yesterday goes unerased—what else is new?
Sure, you're alive, but floored watching the shadowed crawl.
What you choose, what's chosen you—a trade, you think.

Erase the din of yesterday—what isn't new goes.
For you, this dawning: all is clear for one second
and you have a choice—trade out, think. Choose.
Misunderstanding slowly burning in your bones.

All is clear—you're one second to the dawn,
the lingering, glassy world—the lit beyond outside.
Your bones slowly stand in what's burning under
pen & paper. Light mourning a routine of life.

AT SPOFFORD LAKE

The lake is quiet, but if we listen
we can hear the clap of crane wings,
splashes on the water's sleepy face.
Around the small canoe, the fog
holds still. We cast out lines into cloud
riffling the silence. My father and I
say nothing to each other. I watch
my line, try to follow the thread into
and through the brume to where
the water puckers, swallows the hook.
It's hard to see. The bait is gone.
So I listen to him breathe, the boat's sides
balancing against the calm, the space
our voices could have filled if I had said
I was all right with saying nothing.

POEM TO USHER IN THE SEASON

You rise from bed and there's the frost
creeping up the window pane. Cold again. All this
while you slept. It's no one else's fault you missed
those small things—you didn't see it yesterday,
but all those leaves.

You walk the block—
first fires, wood to fleeting ember. Strange specters
floating from the houses. In this still and stunted season,
your body tells you what you couldn't count—breath
alive in air. But it's official when a lone blackbird hops
his balance from the wire, mouth creaking open
like your front door—his signature a lone echo
headed home.

All this happened when?
Stalks gone, earth turned up. No more tobacco flowers—
no more pink-blush petals, pistil spears. Proof positive
that all you make can't be that important after all:
this weather is your word undone another year
in a row and what you thought was clarity
simply just a different color haze.

All the stars
unseen now, closer to going out for good, so you
could miss the point like you did before and before
and before. You should write it down exact—just the way
you want it said:

if I could hold each thing I've named
I'd bring them to my face, kiss them till they booted me away.

AT PLEASANT HILL TO VISIT SHAKERTOWN

Your parents with us for the afternoon
and they don't know we've tried for months.
Even last night we leaned on one another
in the shadows of the kitchen rather than the bed.
Now I wonder what we might have made.

Today the air is crisp, but sun streaks warm
on the plain—October clear bringing families
out to see how people used to live: plows and saws,
fires kept so the faithful wouldn't freeze.
We walk the dusty cut along the fenced fields.

As we go, the wind heaves and points to the graves:
quiet stones and elegies, small remains left back.
And I wonder what we'll leave behind and if you
brought with us a beating heart, tucked away—
another village hiding in these still Kentucky hills.

AFTER CHUCK'S ZEN GARDEN

Dawn: The kitchen window beads with rain and you can hear the wind shouldering the broadside of the house. You look through your window to Chuck's yard where water and air have washed over his grass, his trees, his garden, his little pond. It occurs to you that if Chuck were a Buddhist monk he'd have been up hours ago. But Chuck isn't Buddhist, he's Baptist—he's middle-aged and kind, fleshy and round. He isn't into tangling his legs like a lotus, or centering his breath with gentle *ohhhhhmmmms*. And he may or may not be disciplined enough to be still in the rain hours before sunrise. In fact, his fundamentalism might cause him to frown upon the thought of it, and your ecumenical treatment of his well-planned garden. Instead, Chuck only knows one Noble Truth: *I plant it and God does the rest* he says each time you compliment his grinning tiger lilies, the velvet tufts of starlight moss, and frilly softball-sized chrysanthemums. And maybe he's right, maybe he does nothing. *Sometimes it's what you don't do* he says. You think, now, watching his garden soaked with water that the beds have bloomed because he stayed away. He lets them have the things they want— whiskered light, nutrient soil, and—most easily—a little time. Then your mind snaps, you realize you're anxious, expendable, one needle on Chuck's stoic pine. You sit down at the kitchen table and everything has meaning in its ability to end. You note the music in the wind, the clock behind you counting down each dim second. The world goes on so easily without you. Everything goes on without you—tectonics, volcanic spews, shifting tide, glacial till. Whatever happens now, even as it happens slowly as a growing thumbnail, has one thing in common: the absence of you. Cities get built and babies get born. Light still makes shadow. And so what? The punchline please: the pressure's off; enjoy your day. You look at the rugged stones around the pond in disbelief, the green shafts of soaked flowers, solid like the spokes in a wheel. You thumb your nose and laugh. You smirk—world full circle, laid out like a keen, smiling gift.

YOUR DAYS ARE WAITING

There's certainty made in the calm of a river—a way
steady like the leaves that paper-boat the surface of water.
Even a clamor of hooves throbbing in purple morning light
narrows us—a waking in every wilderness.

But even these things fall asleep inside the mind
and slip away by night.

How will you remember what it's like to stare
into the constant moon? To watch the jet stream's hand
push clouds through dark and stars like nestled ships on the ocean?

Your days are waiting to be left behind.
So now, before sleep makes a single forgetting,
etch in yourself
this moon,
this leaf,
this star.

ACKNOWLEDGEMENTS / NOTES

Special thanks is in order to the journals who first published many of these poems—often in different versions with alternate titles—and to the editors who believed in them:

Blood Lotus: The Hole

The Chrysalis Reader: Natural Order & Northern Cross

Copper-Nickel: At Pleasant Hill to Visit Shakertown & Novena #6

The Cresset: Etymology, In January, & Naming the Stars

The Curator: You Are Sitting in the Kitchen, Only a Witness

Existere Magazine: Novena #1 & #2

In Touch Magazine: At Spofford Lake, On Prayer, Novena #8

Kudzu: Confession

Limestone: Slave Wall

Membra Disjecta: Where Shadows Come From

New Southerner: Your Days Are Waiting

Perspectives: A Journal of Reformed Thought: Novena #5

Relief Journal: Ghost Story, Trigger, & Poem to Usher in the Season

Riverwind: After Chuck's Zen Garden

Rock & Sling: The Jilted Husband Speaks

Ruminate Magazine: To Mark the Place & Novena #3, #4, #7

The Los Angeles Review: Fathom

The Sawmill: Quanta

The Stickman Review: Atropos

The Xavier Review: At Spofford Lake

Windhover: Loving Thy Neighbor & Hallelujah I'm a Bum

Some of these poems appeared in other places as well, including the Red Lion Square podcast, the devotional/Lenten readers from Asbury Seminary, "Abide" and "Descent," the anthology "Needles and Bones" from Drollerie Press (2009), and Tania Runyan's "How to Write a Poem" from T.S. Poetry Press (2015). Poems were also reprinted from two of my previous books "Morning and What Has Come Since" (Finishing Line Press, 2007) and "Making Manifest: On Faith, Creativity, and the Kingdom at Hand" (Seedbed, 2014). Lastly, the most recent poems in this collection were commissioned for L. Callid Keefe-Perry's necessary and brilliant book "Way to Water: A Theopoetics Primer" (Cascade, 2014)—I was honored to be tasked with such an important project.

By name, I'd like to thank Brianna Van Dyke and Leah Maines, whose early belief in my work helped keep me going. Also, my mentors—Fred Smock, Maureen Morehead, Jeanie Thompson, Debra Kang Dean, Molly Peacock, Richard Cecil—were instrumental in helping develop this small body of early work. And especially Rane Arroyo, who is deeply missed.

Several editors, friends, and readers supported me, spent time with these poems, or otherwise kicked my butt along the way, and I'm glad for such folks. Thanks to Brad Fruhauff, Cameron Lawrence, David Wright, Grace Farag, Jae Newman, John James, Karen McDavid, L. Callid Keefe-Perry, Marci Johnson, Nicholas Samaras, Paul Quenon, Reid Bush, Rod Dixon, Susanna Childress, Tania Runyan, & Thom Caraway. I'm sure someone has been forgotten from this litany—and to you I apologize.

Last, thanks to my family—Mom, Dad, Amy, and Evan, who love me without condition; Jim and Ginny, whose support has been tremendous; the Goeller clan, whose care and kindness means so much; and in loving memory of Emil, Emma, Doc, Elsie, and Gilda. And, most of all, to whom this book is dedicated.

/

The title of this book is derived from George Oppen's poem "Blood from the Stone." Otherwise, some individual poems deserve mention for their dedications or necessary information:

"The Jilted Husband Speaks" draws on the myth of Apollo and Coronis. Apollo, after learning of Coronis's infidelity from Corvus—a pure white crow—cursed the bird, turning his feathers black.

"Slave Wall" takes its subject from limestone walls that weave throughout the state of Kentucky. Apparently, slaves mastered this kind of masonry from Irish immigrants who came to the country with the skill of building. Some of these walls are under protection by the state as monuments of heritage.

"Atropos" plays with referents to several different mythologies, theologians, scientists, authors, and philosophers including Plato, Calvin, Bentham, Kant, Sartre, Prisig, Dawkins, and—from the title—The Fates. This poem is for the students and faculty of Lexington Catholic High School, as we mourned our loss of Colin Cox together.

"At Cave Hill Cemetery" is for Amy Munson.

"Etymology" is for David Holzknecht.

"On Prayer #1" riffs on language pilfered from Hebrews 12:18-29.

"Natural Order" is for the Haven and Beals families.

"Hallelujah I'm a Bum" takes its title from Harry McClintock's song and is for Callid, Kristina, and Nahar Keefe-Perry.

"To Mark the Place" is for JD Walt.

"At Pleasant Hill to Visit Shakertown" takes place at Shaker Village in Kentucky. Now nearly extinct, the Shakers are an Anabaptist sect that do not believe in indulging fleshly pleasures, thus abstaining from sex.

"Poem to Usher in the Season" is for Jeremiah Aja.

"Pantoum Breakfast Scramble" is for Michael Winters.

Lastly, I'd like to thank Cascade Books for their work with this project, especially Christian Amondson, who put some serious blood and sweat into making a beautiful book, and has become a trusted and close friend. And finally Don Martin, for his invitation to put together a book, and his endurance in seeing it to print. What you're doing for us is a gift of the highest order, and this book would not have happened if it weren't for your care and attention. Thank you again and again.

www.ingramcontent.com/pod-product-compliance
Lightning Source LLC
LaVergne TN
LVHW041203080426
835511LV00006B/725